Table of Cor...

A Daring Voyage

Lisbon's harbor hummed with activity. Men sweated and strained as they packed supplies into four ships docked there. Captain Vasco da Gama stood close by. He watched the men

Lisbon harbor

with interest. Tomorrow, July 8, 1497, would be a great day for him. Captain da Gama and his crew would leave the safety of Portugal far behind. In the next few months, da Gama hoped to find a sea route to India. He knew that such a discovery would make his nation one of the richest in the world.

Vasco da Gama had been selected for this important voyage by Portugal's young king, Manuel I. The king knew that the voyage to the East would be long and difficult. To lead the mission, he needed a skillful and strong-willed captain. Da Gama seemed to be the perfect choice.

King Manuel I

The Spice Trade

Vasco da Gama was born in about 1460 in Sines, a small town south of Lisbon, and he grew up near the sea. Da Gama was a brave and able seaman, but he was also known to be a

A statue of Vasco da Gama stands in front of a church in the Portuguese port city of Sines.

hard master. He had a hot temper, and could be strict and even cruel. In 1497, da Gama was in his thirties and unmarried: He had no wife or children to worry about during the long months at sea. The king was sure that da Gama was the man to find the spices and other riches in India.

In the late 1400s, spices such as pepper, cinnamon, cloves, and nutmeg were important to people in Europe. There were no refrigerators, so meat was often preserved with salt to keep it from going bad. The spices from India helped mask the taste of salted or decaying meat.

Spices were important to European diners.

A trade caravan travels through Asia.

Italian traders then sold the spices to the rest of Europe at very high prices. King Manuel knew that if Portugal could get the spices directly from India, the prices would be much lower. But the only way to do this was to find a sea route to the east. Since the 1440s, Portugal had been sending ships to try and find a water route to India. But so far, no one had managed to do it.

The spices were brought from India to Egypt, and across the Mediterranean Sea to Italy.

A map of da Gama's voyage

The Saint Gabriel was da Gama's flagship.

Careful Preparation

Da Gama had prepared for his trip for two years. Shipbuilders designed two special ships to make the long journey. These ships were big, three-masted vessels that withstood storms better than other ships of the time. One of the ships, the *Saint Gabriel,* was da Gama's **flagship.** He captained this ship himself. The *Saint Raphael,* the second ship, was commanded by da Gama's brother, Paulo. Two other ships would also make the trip. The *Berrio* was much smaller and faster than the two big ships. The fourth and largest of da Gama's ships was a store ship that held much of the fleet's supplies.

Now, after months of planning, the big day was here. The four ships had been loaded with enough food to last three years. Hard biscuits, water, butter, wine, vegetables, and salted beef, as well as sugar and salt were all loaded into the store ship. Other items, mostly cheap **trinkets,** were packed on board too. These items included copper bowls, glass beads, tin rings, small bells, mirrors, and striped

Ships in Lisbon harbor

cloth. Da Gama hoped to trade these goods for gold and spices in Africa and India.

The crew was made up of about 170 men including a number of convicts who had been sentenced to death. The king had agreed to pardon them if they survived the voyage. These men would perform all the most dangerous tasks. One person on the voyage kept a diary. This diary is the only firsthand account of da Gama's voyage but no one knows who the writer was.

To the Open Sea

On the night of July 7, da Gama and some of his crew entered a tiny church near the harbor. Da Gama, a deeply religious man, spent the evening praying for a successful trip. That same evening, King Manuel gave the explorer a special silk banner.

The banner was a symbol of the king's—and God's—blessing.

The next day, the four ships sailed out of the harbor. Their sails snapped crisply in the sea breeze. In one of the first entries in his diary, the unknown crewman wrote: "May God our Lord permit us to

Vasco da Gama was very religious.

accomplish this voyage in his service! Amen!"

On July 26, the four ships arrived in the Cape Verde Islands, off the African coast. Da Gama and his men spent a week there, gathering firewood and loading more water and fresh meat onto the ships. On August 3, they left the Cape Verde Islands and continued their adventure. The crew didn't know it, but this was the last land they would see for a very long time.

Top: Vasco da Gama's ship. Bottom: The remains of a Portuguese fort at Cape Verde

The crew saw no land for three months.

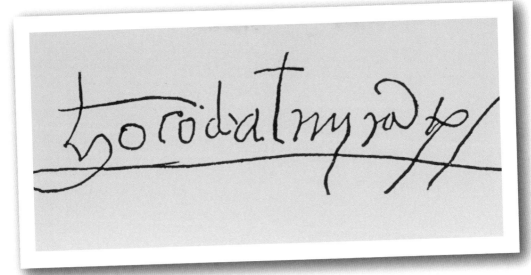

Vasco da Gama's signature

Instead of hugging the African coast, da Gama sailed west, out into the open ocean. For more than three months, da Gama and his men saw no land. Da Gama's exact route through the Atlantic is not known. At one point, however, he may have been within 600 miles (965 kilometers) of Brazil. If so, he was closer to South America than to Africa!

Da Gama's daring was unmatched. The open sea he sailed across was completely unknown and **uncharted.** He had no high-tech instruments to help him find his way and no landmarks to set his course by. Under a less **disciplined** captain, the crew of the four ships might have been afraid. They might have forced the ships to turn back. But da Gama, confident and sure of success, sailed on. He was certain that he would pick up winds from the west that would carry him back to the coast of Africa.

Da Gama's route into the middle of the open ocean may seem strange. But the captain was steering clear of problems that Portuguese sailors had known about for years. Africa's west coast was known for its stormy weather and strong winds and **currents.** By avoiding the coast, da Gama actually shortened his trip. He was the first person to travel a route that sailing vessels still use today.

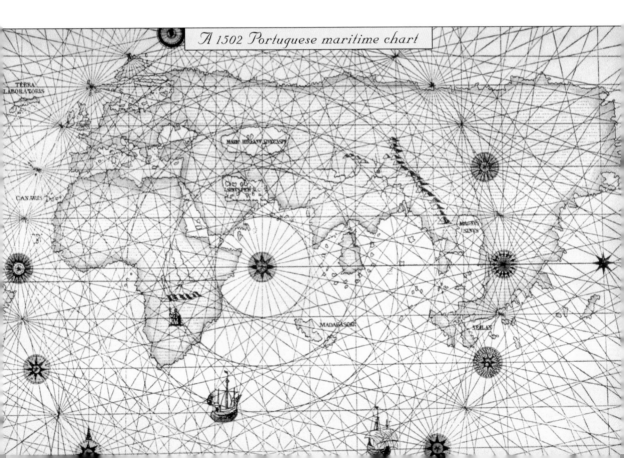

A 1502 Portuguese maritime chart

Back to the Coast

D Da Gama's ships eventually caught the winds he was looking for. These strong sea winds began to blow the ships quickly back to the coast of Africa. On November 1, the crew saw signs of land. On November 4, they reached the African coast.

Da Gama found that he was still about 300 miles (480 km) north of the Cape of Good

A 1502 woodcut depicts ships.

Hope (the southern tip of Africa). Yet he and his men had accomplished an amazing deed. They had covered about 4,000 miles (6,400 km) during the open-sea trip. This trip was the longest such voyage yet taken by Europeans.

On November 7, da Gama and his men made their first stop at St. Helena Bay, in what is now South Africa. There, they repaired the damage done to the ships during the voyage. They mended the sails, scraped the ships' **hulls,** and did other chores. They also gathered wood and freshwater for the

The figurehead of the Saint Raphael

rest of the trip.

At St. Helena Bay, da Gama and his men met native people. At first, the Africans were friendly, but things changed when a member of da Gama's crew tried to visit their village. The Africans attacked, and the captain was wounded in the leg by an arrow. The four ships quickly set sail.

Vasco da Gama

Around the Cape

On November 22, the small fleet of ships finally rounded the Cape of Good Hope. Three days later, da Gama anchored in Mossel Bay. Here, he decided that the store ship was no longer needed. He moved all the supplies off that ship into the smaller ships. He ordered the store ship stripped of all usable parts and

The Cape of Good Hope

A padrão claimed land for the king of Portugal.

then his crew burned the ship's empty hull.

Before leaving Mossel Bay, da Gama put up one of the stone pillars called padrãos that he had brought from Portugal. Each of da Gama's padrãos had Portugal's **coat of arms** carved on it and was topped with a cross. These pillars claimed the land for the king of Portugal.

As the voyage wore on, a disease called **scurvy** took its toll. Scurvy was once a common ailment on long ocean voyages. It is caused by a lack of vitamin C. Without fresh fruits and vegetables, da Gama's men became very sick. Some crew members died.

In late January 1498, the explorers stopped at the Quelimane River in present-day Mozambique. Da Gama called the Quelimane the "River of Good Omens." He put up another padrão here. Da Gama and his men spent nearly a month at the Quelimane. They fixed the ships and traded with the native peoples. The sailors who were sick with scurvy rested and recovered. Then, on February 24, the fleet set sail once again.

Vasco da Gama

Along Africa's East Coast

On March 2, da Gama and his men reached Moçambique, a wealthy Arab trading port, in Mozambique. There, da Gama

This map of Africa was drawn in 1500 after Vasco da Gama's journey.

got his first taste of the riches to be had in the East. In the harbor at Moçambique bobbed four Arab ships filled with goods from India. In his diary, the sailor wrote that the boats were "laden with gold, silver, cloves, pepper, ginger, and silver rings, as also with quantities of pearl, jewels, and rubies, all of which articles are used by the people of this country."

At first, the local ruler was friendly. He agreed to send da Gama two pilots who would guide the Portuguese to India. But when the ruler saw the cheap trinkets that da Gama had brought with him, things changed.

Vasco da Gama

He was insulted. Da Gama was forced to take the two pilots and sail on to Mombasa, in what is now Kenya. Da Gama soon realized he was not welcome there either and, although his pilots jumped ship, da Gama had to move on.

About 60 miles (97 km) to the north lay Malindi, also in Kenya. Malindi's ruler welcomed da Gama and his men. He gave the captain sheep and some pepper and cloves. The ruler also gave da Gama something even more valuable—a pilot. On April 24, with the new pilot at his side, da Gama set off on the last leg of his journey to India.

The ruler of Malindi gave da Gama a pilot to guide him on his journey.

Arrival in India

On May 20, 1498, da Gama and his crew reached Calicut, a town on India's southwestern coast. At that time, Calicut was an important trading center.

Da Gama soon received an invitation to meet the *zamorin*, the ruler of Calicut. The captain and some of his men set out to visit the zamorin in his palace. They were stunned by what they saw.

"The king was in a small court, reclining upon a couch

*Calicut and the coast of southern India
as shown on a map drawn in 1500*

Vasco da Gama met with the zamorin, the ruler of Calicut, in his palace.

gold. So when da Gama showed the ruler the cheap trinkets he had brought from home, the zamorin was not impressed. To make matters worse, Arab traders in the area were trying to poison da Gama's relations with the zamorin. The Arabs did not want to share India's spice trade with the Portuguese.

covered with a cloth of green velvet," according to the diary. "In his left hand the king held a very large golden cup. . . . The canopy above the couch was all **gilt.**"

Calicut's ruler was very rich indeed. He had a beautiful palace, servants, gems, and

As the weeks wore on, da Gama was able to sell some of his goods in the town markets. There he bought samples of spices and jewels to take back to Portugal. Then, in August, da Gama received a letter from the zamorin. The letter, addressed to King Manuel, said, "Vasco da Gama, a gentleman of your household, came to my country, whereat I was pleased. My country is rich in cinnamon, cloves, ginger, pepper, and precious stones. That which I ask of you in exchange is gold, silver, corals, and scarlet cloth."

Da Gama had accomplished his mission. He had reached the East by sea. And he had opened India to trade with the Portuguese. After three long months in Calicut, da Gama could now return home.

A woodcut depicts the spice trade.

The Long Trip Home

The pilot from Malindi had disappeared so da Gama set sail from Calicut on August 29 without him. While the voyage from Africa to India had taken only three weeks, the return trip took nearly three months. The winds were against the small fleet. Storms and periods of dead calm also plagued their journey.

Vasco da Gama

*The Kenyan Cross Monument stands in Malindi, where
da Gama landed on his way to and from India.*

The Cape of Good Hope

Finally, on January 7, 1499, they reached Malindi. There, they were given fresh-water and other supplies. Then they set sail again. In Mombasa, da Gama and his crew were forced to run the *Saint Raphael* aground and burn it. Only fifty-five of da Gama's men had survived—too few to sail all three ships home. Thirty men had died of scurvy on the way back from India.

On March 20, da Gama and his crew once again round-ed the Cape of Good Hope. As they got closer to home, the men began to take heart again. One of the last entries made in the diary reads, "We pursued our route with a great desire of reaching home."

In April, the two ships were separated by a storm. The *Berrio* reached Lisbon on July 10, 1499. Da Gama, however, stopped in the Azores, a group of islands that lie hundreds of miles off the coast of Portugal. There, his brother, Paulo, died and was buried. The *Saint Gabriel* was sent ahead to Lisbon. Da Gama returned to Portugal on a different ship after Paulo's burial, arriving in Lisbon in September 1499. After more than two years and many thousands of miles, da Gama was home at last.

Da Gama's voyage was a great success for Portugal. The end of that voyage marked the beginning of Portugal's

The Azores

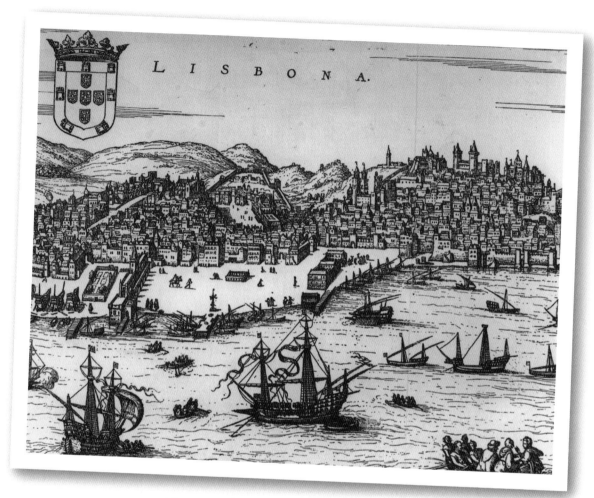

A sixteenth-century view of Lisbon harbor

"golden era." Before long, the small nation was considered the most powerful in the world. The voyage was a success for da Gama too. King Manuel rewarded him with money, land, and fame. Over the years, da Gama became one of the richest men in Portugal.

The Second
Voyage to the East

After the long trip, da Gama married and settled down. For two years, he watched other men sail from Portugal to set up trading centers in the East.

Then, in 1502, King Manuel asked da Gama to return to India. He named the explorer Admiral of the Sea of India. On this second trip, the king

The king named da Gama the Admiral of the Sea of India.

An armed ship

Vasco da Gama and his crew attacked a ship, killing more than 300 pilgrims.

wanted da Gama to show the world Portugal's might and power. And he wanted da Gama to take revenge on the people of Calicut.

Two years earlier, more

than forty Portuguese had been killed by an angry mob in Calicut and King Manuel wanted to make sure this never happened again. He put da Gama in charge of a fleet of twenty ships that were heavily armed with guns and other weapons. Da Gama was told to put the people of Calicut in their place. He was also ordered to destroy the Arab trade in India.

On da Gama's second trip, he showed that he could be cruel. He forced local rulers to give gold to King Manuel. If they hesitated, he threatened them with his ships' big guns. One of da Gama's most

Vasco da Gama could be a cruel man.

terrible acts occurred when he stopped a ship filled with Muslim **pilgrims** going home to India. After taking everything of value from the ship, da Gama locked the passengers below deck and set the ship on fire. About 300 innocent people died.

One of da Gama's last acts of revenge took place in Calicut. The zamorin sent messengers begging da Gama for peace. Da Gama, however, preferred to show Portugal's might. He pointed his guns at the city and opened fire. In two days, da Gama nearly destroyed the port. Then he headed home, his ships loaded with spices and other valuable goods.

For the next twenty years, da Gama saw no active sea duty. Then, in 1524, he was named viceroy, or governor, of India. Da Gama returned to India in September of that year and, two months later, on Christmas Eve, he died. Years later, the body of Vasco da Gama was returned to Portugal to be buried in his homeland.

Many great navigators are buried at this Lisbon monastery
begun in appreciation for da Gama's successful voyage.

Glossary

coat of arms pictures or symbols used to identify a family, a city, or an organization

currents water moving in certain directions

disciplined having self-control

flagship the ship that carries the captain of the fleet

gilt gold

hulls the frames or bodies of ships

pilgrims religious people who travel to a holy place

scurvy a disease caused by lack of vitamin C

trinkets small, cheap objects

uncharted unknown territory; not on any map

Did You Know?

❧ Da Gama's father was supposed to lead the voyage to India but died before he had a chance. Some believe that his brother, Paulo, was then asked to be captain but refused because of poor health. Vasco was the next man asked and he readily agreed to take on the challenge.

❧ Da Gama died in India in December of 1524 but his body was not returned to Portugal until 1538, fourteen years after his death.

❧ At the time of da Gama, spices were used as a means of exchange. For example, you could buy land or pay taxes with spices.

❧ The United States is now the world's largest importer and consumer of spices used to season food products.

Important Dates in da Gama's Life

c.1460
Vasco da Gama
born in Sines,
Portugal

1499
Returns to
Lisbon with
remaining
crew members

1503
Returns to
Portugal after
second voyage
to India

1498
Arrives in
India in May

1524
Named viceroy
(governor) of
India and
returns there
in September
and dies there
in December

1502
King Manuel I
asks him to
return to
India

1497
Da Gama
begins his first
voyage to India
in July

Important People

PAULO DA GAMA (?) brother of Vasco da Gama and captain of the *Saint Raphael* on da Gama's first voyage to India

VASCO DA GAMA (C.1460–1524) Portuguese navigator sent to India by King Manuel I. First western European to sail around Africa to the East.

MANUEL I (1469–1521) King of Portugal from 1495 to 1521

ZAMORIN (?) ruler of Calicut

Want to Know More?

At the Library

Gallagher, Jim. *Vasco da Gama and the Portuguese Explorers.* Broomall, Penn.: Chelsea House, 2000.

Goodman, Joan Elizabeth and Tom McNeely (illustrator). *A Long and Uncertain Journey: The 27,000 Mile Voyage of Vasco da Gama.* New York, N.Y.: Mikaya Press, 2001.

Mattern, Joanne. *Vasco da Gama.* Austin, Tex.: Raintree Steck-Vaughn, 2000.

On the Web

ASTA's World of Spice—The History of the Spice Trade
http://www.astaspice.org/history/history_main.htm
For a history of the spice trade from ancient times to the present

The Sea Route to India and Vasco da Gama
http://www.ucalgary.ca/HIST/tutor/eurvoya/vasco.html
For a history of the search for a sea route to India, including maps

Vasco da Gama Arrives in India
http://campus.northpark.edu/history//WebChron/WestEurope/DaGama.html
For a brief biography of Vasco da Gama

Through the Mail

American Spice Trade Association
560 Sylvan Avenue
P.O. Box1267
Englewood, NJ 07632
201/568-2163
For more information on spices and their use

On the Road

The Mariners' Museum
100 Museum Drive
Newport News, VA 23606
757/596-2222
To see exhibits about navigators and sailors of all kinds

Index

About the Author

Robin S. Doak has been writing for children for more than fourteen
years. A former editor of *Weekly Reader* and *U*S*Kids* magazine,
Ms. Doak has authored fun and educational materials for kids of all
ages. Some of her work includes: *FOSS Science Stories: Mixtures
and Solutions, Human Body, Measurement,* and *Food and Nutrition;
American Immigration; Dark Skies: Alien Invasion* and *The Awakening;
The Associated Press Library of Disasters: Earthquakes & Tsunamis,
Fires & Explosions, Volcanoes,* and *Wild Weather; Pro Sports Hall of
Fame: Hockey.* Ms. Doak is a past winner of an Educational Press
Association of America Distinguished Achievement Award. She lives
with her husband and three children in central Connecticut.